you are so worthy

you are so worthy

saniya kaushal

This is a work of fiction. Names, characters, businesses, places, events, locales, and incidents are either the products of the author's imagination or used in a fictitious manner. Any resemblance to actual persons, living or dead, or actual events is purely coincidental.

ISBN: 978-1-7772299-4-8 (paperback)

Illustrations and cover design by Saniya Kaushal
First printing edition 2022.

Published by Saniya Kaushal
www.saniyakaushal.com

for anyone in search of their worth

for anyone who feels like an imposter

for anyone who feels alone in their battles

my rocks

your love gives me the strength and

courage to tell my stories

thank you to my cherished three

and to my chosen family

table of contents

bruised

her thoughts move quickly
emotions even faster
they come and go before she can catch them

but when she writes
she is forced to acknowledge them
to slow them down
to feel them
to grow from them

writing is her therapy

by giving you the opportunity to experience life
without me
do i risk you forgetting the love you have for me
and getting used to a life without me in it
will i soon be a distant piece of your memory
instead of an active part of your life?

oh some days
i crave to be hugged
by the ones who love me the most
i wish i could teleport
back to you

these video calls
cannot offer me the warmth
or the reassuring love
found in your hugs
that is what i yearn for
in times like these
because sometimes
it gets lonely leaning on myself

everyone was feeding me love
and taking pride in me
but as i received the kind wishes
i was overwhelmed with guilt
i began to feel like
i was accidentally lying to the people i love
deceiving them
because they seemed to see me so much better
than i felt i actually was

when it enters my mind
it rushes in so fast
and overtakes my rational
every ounce of me begins to question
why am i here
how did i get here
do i even belong here

i minimize myself to something so little
that i can physically feel the desperation
to do better
to be better
to feel better

this is the dangerous game of self-doubt
that my brain wrestles with

an average task
sometimes takes him over twice the length
because he is fixated on precision and perfection

the fear of failing drains him

she is just trying not to burn out
on the journey to her dreams

why is it so hard for him
to conceptualize
his own capabilities?

his thoughts never fail to leave him
feeling inferior
to the people who surround him

they do not understand
the stress of this internalized doubt
how i genuinely feel
that this is a fluke
that i'm here because i'm lucky
not because i'm deserving

how do i keep showing up
every single day
pretending i feel like i am worthy of being here
will this charade get easier with time?

always the worst
right after my birthday
as i reflect on all the praise
and compliments
that i feel
i so wrongly received

you are so worthy

oh gosh
the praise
how it drives me to feeling the greatest guilt

if only they knew how unworthy of it i really was
how am i fooling everyone except for myself?

just for a day
i crave to understand
the feeling of believing
that i have earned my accomplishments
that i belong in my roles
that i am not the product of a series of flukes
that i am actually worthy

i want to believe this is imposter syndrome
but i fear that i am just the imposter

that never-satisfied mentality
leads me to great ambitions
but robs me of any self-pride

it was so subconscious
he didn't mean to do it
but he always did
comparing himself to others
always placing himself at the bottom
inferior to all

he could prove it to himself
a million times and more
yet still not fully have faith in himself

the tornado looms
it spirals over me
a combination of fears
insecurities
and disappointments in myself
why does it take me longer?
why do i find it harder?
what am i doing here?

the delay
between the tireless work
and the desired results
is the real test

sometimes he wondered
how it felt
to be loved by someone
with no obligation to him

she was ashamed to admit
that the lack of his affection
translated to her believing
she was not worthy
because she was not enough

sleepless nights
nauseating mornings
intrusive thoughts
as he awaits results day
the fear of failure consumes him

but if we are all up against the same challenges
enduring the same hardships
why do they seem less anxious
less stressed
why am i slower
what am i missing
i don't deserve to be here
they're going to realize it soon too

they assume he is invincible
so he is robbed of any support
if only they knew how afraid he actually is
how despite there being so many people around him
he still feels so isolated
he still feels so lonely
he craves a listening ear
but is never offered one

part of me hopefully convinces myself
that this cannot all just be luck
that i must be doing something right

until another piece overshadows
and i remain reluctant to accept
that i am deserving

why is it that every time someone tells me
they're proud of me
i search for why they shouldn't be

why every time someone praises my
accomplishments
i remind them of my failures

why every time i get a compliment
i explain all that i am missing

the desperation to feel a sliver of worth
so she can push herself forward
to take on another day

he is fearful
so he puts it off
because he knows
he can’t carry the feeling
of falling short
yet again

as if the task isn't daunting enough
she bears the fear
rooted by the nerves
of being exposed as a fraud

she described me as “cool as a cucumber”
little did she know
that in that moment
this cucumber
felt like she was being emotionally deep fried
in fear that her cover
was about to be blown

"it must come easy"
most certainly not
what's pictured is the product
you have not a clue of the equation
it took to get there

you will never understand
the emotional exhaustion
the intrusive self-battles
the internal wars
the broken hopes
and the resilient fights
that turned up on the way

if anyone spoke to me
the same way i sometimes speak to myself
i'd file a restraining order

absorbed by self-doubt
his mind quickly becomes an enemy
instead of an ally
he becomes physically sick
dizzy in the thoughts convincing him
he doesn’t deserve to be here

the pressure
of using his own judgement
in a way that did not withhold him
but also did not emotionally endanger him
drove him confused and exhausted

and sometimes i fall victim
to the same toxic behaviours
i beg others
not to use towards each other
but still choose to use
on myself

i'm begging myself to believe
that i've earned my spot here
that i deserve to be here
that i'm worthy of being here

i feel like a hypocrite
for preaching kindness to others
but at times
being so degrading of myself

all we ever showed
were the highlights

it is hard to conceptualize
the adversities
if you are not living them
especially when we masked things so nicely

how can we blame you
for assuming
nothing was wrong?

this collection of individuals
disguising their internal screams and battles
with external smiles
concealing their strength and resilience
because they would rather just appear
perfectly unshaken

the fear of appearing weak
the desire of protecting his ego
leads him to burying his vulnerabilities
and presenting as perfectly content

those who surround him are fooled by his mask
so they are left feeling inadequate
questioning themselves
why do they feel these emotions that he is immune to
why aren't they as strong as he is
their low self-confidence drops even deeper

no one is leaning on each other for support
because no one wants to share that they are suffering
this painful cycle continues

your tough act
it’s like looking in a mirror
trying to conceal our fears in fake smiles
and false hopes

how are we supposed to feel like we are not isolated
in our thoughts
when society rewards masking ourselves
as invulnerable figures
everyone must appear okay
even when we are not

beneath the hard front
she feels the same emotions
she suffers the same pains
she's just better at disguising them

she convinced herself
to expect the worst
in hopes of protecting her heart
from painful disappointment

being surrounded by people who refuse to demask
their struggles
can be damaging sometimes
it makes you feel alone
and self-loathing
of your inability to present a happy face
like everyone else does

why was the turbulence
shattering him
more than his neighbours

perhaps it came down
to the broken foundation
he kept trying to neglect
as he buried it in layers

it could no longer withstand
the same pressure
because he refused to fix it

watching you suffer in silence
but play the happy character outside
pains me
isn't it exhausting having to hide your emotions
why don't you feel like you deserve support?

i never want you to experience fear
when all you have ever done
for my entire life
is save me from the darkness
and try to shield me from pain
i hope my presence can be even half as consoling
as yours

you are so worthy

his love pours out
to those he supports

his unwavering presence
no matter the distance

he is always encouraging
despite his own adversities

he is always the one they can count on

i can only hope he receives the kindness that he gives
that is what he truly deserves

how can someone i love so much
hate themselves so deeply
how are they so blind to all the traits
that i admire so greatly
how can i prove to them that they are worthy?

the pain you have had to endure
it is not fair
it hurts my heart thinking about
what it must have done to you

you are so much stronger
than you give yourself credit for

what good are the standards
you set for others
when you treat yourself so poorly?

you belittle yourself
continuously
why?

you are so worthy
of so much more

i desire to feel adequate
but somehow i stay in my own way
i am my own obstacle
in my fight
to feeling worthy enough

so this is what they mean
when they describe a love-hate relationship
how i want something so deeply
but nothing has ever made me feel so worthless
how the gratification is unmatched
but the process drains me
how there is nowhere else i would rather be
but sometimes staying feels impossible

i grasp so tightly
insecure and in fear
of you slipping away

because you don’t realize
how dependent i became
on your consistent support
when you got up and left
without explanation
i questioned every inch of my identity
to unravel
what drove you away

she desperately yearns to understand
what she is lacking
what makes her unappealing

why does no one wish
to make her theirs?

she has given you the reins to have this effect on her

removing her guard to feel your love
has also given you access to show her pain
she can only hope that by removing her brick walls
they don't end up trampling her

the inconsistency
varied more than a sine wave
it became an addiction
tirelessly chasing the highs
and finally reaching the maximums
only to helplessly sink down to the lows

these books have become my journals
where i can pour out my reflections and observations
and process my joys and disappointments
as i witness the world evolve around me
and experience the evolution of myself

but what i didn't realize
was that every time i opened up
and shared my vulnerabilities
i was helping to sharpen the knife
that would eventually
stab me in the back

i forgot how hurtful
being vulnerable can become
thank you for reminding me
to be more cautious when i open up

we repeatedly accept so much less
than what we deserve
because we repeatedly assign ourselves
such poor worth
through our degrading self-talk and criticism

she didn’t want to think
she was trusting too quickly

she wanted to believe
she was safe from judgement

and so she turned a blind eye to all the red flags
until those became the only things she could see

she regretted being so naïve
for assuming the kindness she received
was genuine
lacking ill intentions
free from conditions

once again
she learned the hard way
that she had trusted too quickly

how did i place myself so low
to fully believe
that the way i was treated
was all that i deserved?

i'm allowed to stop trusting you
if you've given me a reason
stop trying to guilt me
stop trying to gaslight me

how have you magically become the victim?

if i showed even half the caution
when trusting others
that i do
when trusting myself

the bar became so low
for what he convinced himself he deserved
that even attention in the form of disrespect
brought him fulfilment

i really wish i didn't have to overthink
someone showing me kindness
and that i could just embrace love
without contemplating its motives
but my past experiences have taught me differently
that maybe i'm not deserving
i've had my trust shattered
and my faith tainted

isn't it ignorant not to learn from my mistakes?

our craving for affection
invades our common sense
we know this is going nowhere
but in this moment
it fulfills us
so we mindlessly continue
ignorant of the painful consequences
that undeniably await us

i'm afraid that by allowing you
to feed me this much joy
i'm also giving you the power
to drain me empty
by unexpectedly withdrawing the kindness
you were once so quick to give me

he was surrounded by affirmations
yet somehow
the disapproval of just one
was enough
to drown him
in self-loathing disgust
insecurities
and feelings of worthlessness

this was not what he deserved

my forgiveness is my downfall
it turns me into a victim
of being taken advantage of
time and time again

they assume i will never leave
so they neglect the way they treat me

i am afraid to abandon them
so despite being taken for granted
i always stay

they perceived my differences
as reasons
to devalue me
to deem me inferior
and to degrade my identity

the same one i had finally grown so proud of

please
sound it out
the way i have explained
syllable by syllable
with the same respect i showed when i learned yours

please
ask me if you are not sure
i wish to be addressed
by the name my parents lovingly chose for me
not by the lazy attempts
you have decided my name's origin is worth

unfortunately
it is a deeply rooted
engravement in our society
that we will have to work harder
day in day out
to prove we are not inferior
due to the colour of our skin
we will never outgrow this reality

this is not self-pity
or hatred towards you because of your privilege
this is acceptance
and motivation
to prove that the sentencing society has wrongfully
given to my race
is misguided and ignorant

finally
the representation
we craved growing up
is slowly appearing

i can finally identify
with the admirable protagonist
instead of the shameful side character

these beauty standards
that were never built for us
are becoming more inclusive

although this is the bare minimum
i praise it as a success
because these are luxuries
we never had
when we needed them the most

all of our beautiful dolls
and favourite movie princesses
looked the same
nothing like us

how were we ever supposed to grow
to feel worthy enough
when the odds were always against us?

this subconscious fear
that if i revealed too many of my differences
shared too much of my culture
i would be left on the outside

i was the minority
trying to take on a mountain
of demeaning stereotypes
so it was easier to temporarily assimilate

the regret of not standing proud
the guilt of not using my identity to educate
has overwhelmed me

i was just a kid

how does someone who took so much from me
against my will
have the audacity
to ask for me to give him more willingly
these expectations infuriate me

i despise this feeling of anger
that i can feel rising inside of me
i am further frustrated that you have driven me
someone who always strives to feel brightness
to sink in this darkness

some days
you make it so damn hard
to be the bigger person

i sincerely wish you the best
so your misery does not drive you
to deflect your pain onto others
as you did with me

why do you feel so entitled
to treat people so cruelly
oblivious to the consequences?

what are you trying to prove?

you attempted to use
the pieces of glass
you had collected
from shattering the hearts of others
to repair your own

how did that work out for you?

how dare you lack so much compassion
towards a cause
that takes so many lives
and shatters so many others

forced to conceal half of his identity
to obey the deep-rooted norms
established by his culture
i hope for him that soon
he will be able to express himself freely
without feeling shame
for the same traits
which i think make him so beautiful

so ready to inflict their opinions on me
so ready to inflict their judgements
what they do not realize is
just because i am different from them
it does not mean i am broken

fueled with anger
from people who treat their success as superiority
granting them the right
to demean anyone
whom they view as “less”

success to you may be measured by perfect resumes
but success to us was prioritizing mental health
and supportive relationships
so before assuming that we have failed
perhaps appreciate that we each have the right
to our own variations

surrounded by these adults
who seem to believe
they would do a better job at raising us
than our parents
respectfully, please back off
we are proud of who we are
we do not need your concern
or your insulting attempts at trying to "fix" us

maybe i received it wrong
but maybe you just shouldn’t have said it

she hung her privilege
over his head
as if it gave her some kind of authority
to treat him
as nastily
as she wished

i don't understand
why you think that your upbringing
allots you the right
to disrespect mine

when you disrespect my upbringing
you are disrespecting my parents
who spend every single day
trying to enrich their little girl
into a strong and powerful woman

i may listen silently as you degrade me
but i will never tolerate you degrading them

just because we were raised differently
it does not mean i was raised wrong

i'm sick of you passing assumptions
judging my actions
ridiculing my expressions
shaming my apparel
and ignoring my values

you label me as a disgrace to my culture
and insult the way my parents have raised me

well let me remind you of the way
i love them so deeply
and how with each year of life
i grow even more grateful
that they have bloomed me happy
and prioritized my well-being over a pressure
to comply with traditional norms

perhaps our world looks different from yours
but this does not mean we are at fault

and if they are proud of my identity
i will be seeking no approval from you
for you have not even tried to unravel my layers
meanwhile, they are the formula behind my existence

you are so worthy

she fed kindness to my face
just to relentlessly attack who i was
in my absence

for goodness' sake
when will you understand that
the lifestyle you were raised in
the luxuries you possess
the financial balance of your family
does not grant you the right
to treat others as inferior

you are so worthy

every day you would feed me lies

i don't understand
why humanity feels
they have the right
to lay judgements
on a person's entire life
in a matter of minutes

they do not know the battles she has fought
they do not know the struggles he has encountered
they do not know the resilience she has demonstrated
they literally do not know anything about him

she tried so hard to focus on herself
and mind her own business
but you made it your mission
to involve yourself
by spreading your judgements
on different aspects of her life

why?
for what reason?
what did you gain
by costing her so much?

just because i do not confront you
it does not mean i am not hurting
or that i do not feel betrayed
beyond repair

it simply means that i no longer have the energy
to invest time into people
who repeatedly hurt me
behave fake to my face
and go out of their way
to make me feel inadequate

these games
they confuse me
i wish i could just speak my mind
and do as i feel
without fear of not mirroring your behaviours
appropriately

they thought they knew her story
they had been around her for years
but they only observed what she chose to reveal
she kept her traumas guarded
they saw her exactly how she wished to be seen
she chose not to share her pains
so she just played along happily
as they all envied her “perfect” life

when will people realize
there is more than one route
there is more than one image
there is more than one identity
that can feed into the same result?

oh how quick they were to assume
an entire upbringing
an entire character
an entire lifestyle
just from a few photos on a feed

the trauma he witnessed as a child
slowly began creeping up on him
affecting the way
he trusted
loved
and valued himself

he was living
in the shadows
of the ghosts of his past
that he had helplessly tried
so hard to combat

she hides her pain in jokes and laughter
no one would ever imagine
the layers of trauma she is working through

one can never tell a person's interior
from solely observing their outside

it was heart-shattering to watch
how he despised himself more every day

how each time he let his guard down
and allowed his emotions to show
he feared he looked so weak

meanwhile
as he loathed what he thought was fragility
all we could see
was inspirational strength and resilience

can you blame him for always being on the run
when every time he opens up
he gets manipulated to the point
of just wanting to stay shut

"it is nice of you to invest in your daughters"
as if we should be deemed unworthy and undeserving
have our potential ruled out
we are the same daughters who greet you so kindly
our dreams are just as big

my parents stood in disbelief
as they once again received
unwanted pity
for having no sons
when they love their girls so dearly

how many more times
would we have to accommodate
these backwards beliefs
to save peace?

bandaged

the unwavering faith you have in me
reignites my strength
recharges my perseverance
convinces me i am capable
because if you love me so unconditionally
i must be worth something

how i’ve watched you rebuild your life
using the shards of glass
that once made you bleed
you resculpted your identity
using these experiences
to help you grow
instead of discarding them completely

you are now shining brighter than ever
carrying out the life you had once deemed impossible
achieving the dreams
you had originally convinced yourself
you were incapable of

your resilience is incredible
i am in awe of you

i don't want a part in this masquerade ball
where we must present as emotionless characters
incapable of fear
pain
and sadness
these emotions define our journeys
and overcoming them defines our progress

we are not only as valuable
as the number of messages we received that day

you have shown me
what a support system is
reminded me
how unconditional love feels
fed laughter
into days that felt dark and overwhelming
thank you for never leaving my side

i was afraid
that if i left
my presence would be forgotten
my personality would not be craved
out of sight
out of mind
but you guys have taught me
what true, authentic, loyal relationships are
there has never been a day
even though i've been millions of miles away
that i've been deprived of your care
thank you for teaching me
what unwavering support feels like

but maybe if we all shared our vulnerabilities
we would all come to realize
that we're not alone in our battles
that our struggles do not make us inferior
they only make us human

they call me weak
for pouring out my personality
to strangers
for sharing my insecurities
on the internet
for writing books
about my battles
but i’m just trying to normalize
these feelings

as she hugs me
for a moment
some of the endless belief she has in me
trespasses into my mind
giving me temporary hope
that i am worthy of my accomplishments
and capable of handling my future

proud of how far i’ve come
but cognizant of the growth i need to make

i deserve to be here
i deserve to be here
i deserve to be here

at the end of the day
there is no place i would rather be
i will get back up
every time
and keep trying until i succeed
because the passion that burns inside of me
far exceeds the forces that try to burn me down

he wouldn't trade this opportunity
for a peace of mind

fulfilled

happy

and complete

this is why

we're doing what we're doing

why we wake up every day

and try harder than the last

we're reminded yet again

that the good outweighs

the bad

she doesn’t know how long it will last
but in this moment
it all feels worth it
she finally feels like she belongs

i am slowly proving to myself
that i am capable
my actions are beginning to speak louder
than the toxic words i feed myself

slowly but surely
we found it reassuring
as we became conscious of the fact
that this feeling of inadequacy
was not an individualized sentence
it was shared by us all

you are allowed to be simultaneously frustrated whilst passionate and determined

it has to be a collective decision
to all show strength in vulnerability
so we can create a safe space for one another

you have supported me in more ways
than you can understand
never underestimate the depths your words can travel
they have helped me unplant seeds of doubt
that would have grown to consume me

those core moments of joy and happiness
when the laughter is literally pouring
out of my intestines
they make my problems feel so minuscule
and unhook me from my fixated stress

those are the moments that keep me going

sometimes my goals feel like my biggest enemies
constantly humbling me
feeding me sources of self-doubt and inadequacy

however, i would rather be tested to grow
than remain satisfied in stagnation

at the time
all he felt was pain
but in retrospect
he realized
those stabbing moments had shaped him
and now
he had grown proud
of the person they had made him

a sleepless night
a restless morning
i opened the page
to view my results
i began to sob
in disbelief
that maybe i was actually capable
and i did deserve to be here
that all my tireless days and nights
were amounting to the progression
of my dreams coming true
it was finally paying off
it was all worth it
this was the closest i had felt
to feeling like i was competent

as heavy as it may bear
this pain is temporary
it is part of a journey
that is strengthening you
enhancing your character
and building your resilience
until you finally reach
your longer-lasting joy

please never mistake my exhaustion for my surrender
i am allowed to grow tired
during this long journey
but remain unwavering
in my determination and will
as i continue my fight for my dreams

through the stress and the tears
he reminded himself
that he has never regretted
fighting for his future
for every day was bringing him closer
to finally grasping his goals

she looks forward to continuing to grow into herself
to forming her new identity in this field
to allowing herself to be impressed
with her achievements
to feel deserving of her spot
to feel belonging in her role
to finally believing she is enough

all those days
i thought i couldn't continue
i thought i needed a new route
but forced myself to carry on
had i stopped
i would have deprived myself
of the self-worth
i have since proven i deserve

he needs to stop feeling relieved
when he succeeds
and start to feel deserving

my full-circle moment
when we met face to face
but for the first time
i stood with confidence
unphased and undefeated
no longer seeking your approval
or validation
because now
you hold no power over me

so selfless
so beautiful
her kind heart radiates
amongst everyone she sees

she inspires me
the way i have watched her gain confidence
and finally, acknowledge her worth and capabilities
embracing her success without questioning
how she achieved it

i love this for her
she deserves to feel worthy
i want her never to feel anything less

watching your ambitious
and grinding mentality
has taught me to never let my thoughts restrict me
and to never let my dreams become bounded
you are my living proof
that anything is possible

though it was painful
by stepping down from that situation
she knew
she was stepping up for herself
in a way that no one else could

you are so worthy
of so much more
than you give to yourself

don't stop until you feel it
until you truly believe it
until you can finally own your self-worth
without feeling guilty

appreciating your value does not make you
narcissistic

you need to bandage the bruises
your self-criticism has allowed
to breed
inside your head

why does their success
frustrate you?
can’t you use their wins as motivation
instead of as fuel for your anger?
why don’t you use this energy to build yourself up
instead of trying to tear them down?

i promise you
there's a deeper root
to this uncalled-for hatred
you've developed
for an undeserving stranger

instead of projecting your insecurities
into vile attacks on innocent people
nurture yourself
prioritize your growth
enrich your life without damaging others

in a time overwhelmed by stress
uncertainty
fear
and loneliness
every kind gesture
every encouraging word
every thoughtful action
gave her momentum
to carry on
to the next day
so please never underestimate
the ripple effects
that your love to others can begin
it can save days
it can save happiness
it can save motivation
it can even save lives

care for your soul
no one else will
the way that you can

if we all began to vocalize
our individual silent battles
perhaps we'd feel less at war with ourselves
and more like we're all just human

we have so much more in common
than our egos allow ourselves to show

comparison
can kill dreams
if you let it

but what if
instead of using our vulnerabilities as ammunition
against each other
we helped bandage each other up
to send us all into battle stronger next time

when we treat ourselves like dirt
we will actively seek nothing more
than what we feel we deserve

not a rotten apple amongst a perfect basket
there is beauty in your bruises

those people who look like
they've got it all under control
they think the same about you
doubt does not leave any of us untouched

the love they give
is not always the love you deserve
don't restrict the affection you receive
to the maximum they can provide

you will not sugarcoat your way out of this one
i will not let you

i do not understand your ego
who are you trying to prove yourself to
what will that gain for you
all you are doing is separating us
when we could be so much stronger in harmony

who decided we have to treat each other like this
can’t we change the narrative
does it have to be too late?

start to convince yourself
that you are worthy
of your praise

you are intimidated by her
she is intimidated by the world

no one is as fearless as they seem

what is the point of pretending we don't feel
these dynamic emotions
humans are meant to feel things
what are we trying to prove by swaying from this?

"i'm the only one who feels this way, they do not"
darling, those same people think the same about you
these challenges pinch us all
but we refuse to let it show
in fear of looking weak
when this is what actually helps us grow

here is your reminder
that we do not have to let
the hurtful labels we've been assigned
cloud our judgments of ourselves

i wish she could see herself
through the lens of another eye
the same parts of her body she hates so adamantly
are the same parts we find so beautiful

i go hard for the people i love
i'm not sure you deserve that anymore

this external validation will never fill the gap
of where your internal beliefs should lie
liberate yourself

i want to give you hope and reassurance
that you are never alone in these battles
there is so much support out there
in so many different forms

conflicts are fought stronger as a team
solo resources and support
will never outweigh a collective effort

okay, but look how much you've conquered
and achieved
since the last time
you thought you couldn't carry on
please don't give up now

in reality though, what growth does this masked face
even achieve for you?

you are so worthy
of giving yourself the right
to feel your pain
and share your woes

unburden yourself from the pressure
to dress in invincibility
to silence your anguish

because how are you supposed to grow
well-nourished
without unrooting those rotten weeds

these people you are sabotaging your own
mental health
to impress
remain too fixated in their own lives
to observe yours

it is not worth it

you are so worthy

the beliefs that consume you
the self-berating criticism
the racing insecurities
the feelings of being a hoax
that you've convinced yourself you're feeling alone
i want you to know that you are not

we are trying to fool each other
but in reality
we are only fooling ourselves
by hiding from our emotions
and running away from the opportunities
to overcome them
and come out stronger

don’t let society
minimize you down
to just a figure
ignoring the entire character
that makes you different
your quirks
your fears
the way you love
all of the unique parts about you

each tiring day
as much as it batters you down
as much as it drains you
is bringing you nearer
to forming the reality
and living out those dreams
you have always fantasized about

some days we wake up feeling unstoppable
some days we wake up feeling incapable
every single day we wake up and grind

you are so worthy
of living your life
in your true identity
freely
without fear or constraint
outside of the box
that they have tried to confine you in

and i think if you found
those same positives
that you're getting from these sources of pain
in other areas
it would bring you a lot more peace and happiness

thank you

thank you
for reading
as i once again shared
my raw vulnerabilities

after my first book
i was so nervous to see
how people would resonate with me
but i was gifted with such overwhelming support
i cannot begin to express my gratitude

the world may feel daunting at times
but you have the strength to succeed
and on those days when it may feel harder
please reach out
there are so many resources
so many souls who want to help you
you never need to bear these issues alone

you are so worthy
of any support you need

ps i love to see how readers

connect with my poems

so if you share on social media

please tag me

@saniya.kaushal

About the Author

Saniya Kaushal is a daughter, sister, friend, student, poet, and author of poetry books *you are not ugly* and *you are so worthy.* She is grateful for the opportunity to share her experiences and observations through her writing while raising awareness for subjects close to her heart. Kaushal is a firm believer that there is strength in vulnerability. She is the founder of the *you are not ugly foundation* – a non-profit organization aiming to raise awareness and empower people to overcome their insecurities. Kaushal is soon beginning her third year of medical school.

Kaushal released her first poetry book *you are not ugly,* in 2020. It was inspired by her own experiences growing up being labelled as "ugly" and watching others around her being called derogatory terms. It was her attempt at raising awareness for the damage that thoughtless behaviours can cause. She also wanted to help build the confidence of her readers. It is available as a paperback and e-book worldwide.

More information on Saniya's books and non-profit organization can be viewed online at her website www.saniyakaushal.com.

Printed in Great Britain
by Amazon

25358843R00118